GW00891372

To, Ethel

Get Out the Good China

Mary Higgins

Mary Higgins.

*Wishing you all good things
and blessings in 2009*

SUMMER PALACE PRESS

First published in 2008 by

Summer Palace Press
Cladnageeragh, Kilbeg, Kilcar, County Donegal, Ireland

Printed by Nicholson & Bass Ltd.

A catalogue record for this book is available
from the British Library

ISBN 978-0-9560995-3-2

This book is printed on elemental chlorine-free paper

*to the memory of my husband Vincey
and for my children and grandchildren*

Acknowledgments

Some of the stories in this book have previously appeared in anthologies of the Ballymena Writers' Group: *Maine Lines* (1994); *Fact, Fiction and Folly* (2002); *Blarney With Genius* (2004) and *All Write on the Night* (2005).

The Summer Palace Press is grateful to the Higgins family for helping to collate these stories and especially to Claire for typing the script and Peter for his assistance with the graphics.

Biographical Note

Mary Higgins was born in Ballymena and has lived there all her life. A founder member of the Ballymena Writers' Group, she has told her stories in Ballymena, at the Force 12 Writers' Weekend, Belmullet, County Mayo, and at writers' festivals in Ballina, Castlebar and Edgworthstown, County Longford. At the Four Swans Festival in Ballycastle, County Antrim, Kathleen McGarvey and she sang and told stories on the buses. For many years Mary has contributed to the Ballycastle Writers' *Let Me Take You To the Island* Festival on Rathlin Island, and she was invited to tell her stories in Atlanta and Kentucky, USA.

CONTENTS

Sunday's Child

The child that is born on the Sabbath day shall be bonny and blithe and good and gay. The day I was born was a Sunday and according to my family I didn't live up to any of this, so the saying died a natural death.

'If one of you so much as looks at her when she comes downstairs, it will be God help you.' According to my brothers and sisters these were familiar words used by my mother before my entrance in the mornings. I don't recall these days but five to one is pretty damning and they are all agreed that I was a very cross child.

My brother remembers that I always opened the door to the kitchen crying. 'What's wrong with you, Mary?' Mammy would ask.

'Joey pushed me,' I'd wail.

Swift to clear his name Joey would say, 'I never touched her, Mammy.'

'Well he was going to,' I'd say. 'Sheila's eating the piece of toast I wanted'; 'Anna's sitting on my favourite chair'; 'Joey knows the light is shining in my eyes because he pulled the blind up.' The list was endless.

My eldest sister was the only one who wouldn't have drowned me, given the chance. She would always say, 'Take my seat. Have my toast,' but apparently that wasn't what I wanted. I just wanted to be miserable.

One Sunday morning my Daddy's uncle was sitting in our house and my Mammy was getting me ready for Mass. She was brushing my hair and I was wriggling and whining that she was rugging me. I twisted so much I knocked the brush out of her hand. Uncle Mickey looked at her and said, 'Annie, put her in a sack and take her to the park dam and I swear to God I'll tell nobody.'

I was a very healthy child, which was lucky, as I was absolutely terrified of doctors. Somehow I had got it into my head that they lived just to put you into hospital, where they gave you iodine and you died. Because of this I was scared stiff to get my hair washed. I was sure that if I got soap into my eyes I'd have to go to the doctor and that would be the end of me. I didn't trust anyone to wash my hair except Aunt Lizzie. She was my mother's sister and a patient, good-natured woman and she agreed to come up every Friday night to wash it for me. With promises not to use soap and me armed with a thick towel pressed tight to my eyes, the ritual would begin.

'Are you sure you're not using soap, Aunt Lizzie?'

'No darlin', I'm not.'

'Well, how are you getting it clean then?'

'I'm using *Lux*, pet.'

Mammy and Aunt Lizzie had convinced me that *Lux* wasn't soap. It was kept hidden from week to week. Anna, my sister, was tempted many a time to tell me I was being conned, but the threat of what would happen to her if she did, kept her mouth closed.

One night my Daddy jokingly said to my Mammy, 'Annie, let's take her up and get her christened over again,' the belief being that anyone named Mary was meant for sorrow.

Mammy thought she'd consult the family doctor. 'Doctor Brogan says it's a cycle. He says she'll change when she is seven,' she told Daddy.

'For heaven's sake, we'll all be in the asylum by then.'

The strange thing was that as soon as I entered the school door I became a most obedient child. I was leader of the group and loved telling stories to make them laugh. But come home time, I'd revert back to the Mary my family knew.

One day a girl in my class couldn't get her nib out of her pen and she asked for my help. I put it between my teeth and pulled. I succeeded and the class cheered. Flushed with success, I said, 'It was nothing,' and then realised I'd swallowed the nib. My teacher, who was coming up the corridor, heard the blood-curdling scream I let out, and leapt into the classroom. The girls were all standing round me in a circle, crying to my screaming. When Sister Josephine eventually sorted out what had happened she sent for my eldest sister Nellie to come and take me home. The convent school had a long avenue leading to it, add to that three streets to our front door and 'til the day she died, Mammy swore she heard me screaming and crying from the classroom until the minute I entered the house.

She had to drag me forcibly to the doctor. Mammy told him what had happened and he told me to sit in the waiting room and he took Mammy into the surgery and closed the door. He said 'I didn't want Mary to hear this. The cure is a little unpleasant, but we have to try and ensure the nib does no damage or at least as little as possible. She'll have to take porridge mixed with cotton wool, twice daily, for ten days.'

I was sure he was making arrangements to get me into hospital, so I started kicking the door and shouting, 'I'm not going to the hospital, and I'm not taking iodine.'

Dr. Brogan said 'I see what you mean about Mary's temper.'

Mammy said 'That's nothing to what it will be when she has to take this porridge!' The only way she could get me to take it was to give it to Tommie and Anna as well.

Summer holidays had two highlights. One was a day to Portrush and the second, to Carnlough. My mother always explained that these two outings were so that we'd have something to write about when we were back at school faced with essays on 'Where I spent my Summer Holidays'. The memories we had of both places were of homemade sandwiches and minerals which somehow always seemed to be mixed with sand. The highlight for my mother was the family photographs. There would always be one of us girls with our dresses tucked inside our knickers. She would carefully arrange us with our backs to the sea, the smallest, me, at the front, and then she'd say, 'Smile and pretend you're enjoying yourselves.' Mammy said they were the only times I smiled until the age of seven.

Sing It Loud

My sister Anna was lying in bed with rheumatism pains. Two nuns came to see her and I remember Mammy taking me in to meet them. I had on a red coat and leggings and I said to them, 'Anna hid her comics below the cover before you came in,' and then I said, 'I can sing. Will I sing now?' and before they could say *yes* or *no* I started into singing *Amy Johnson Flew in an Aeroplane*.

I remember the small fire burning in the grate and I can see very plainly the wicker chair my mother lifted me up on to, to sing. I wanted to sing another song, *Show Me the Way to Go Home*, but my mother took me, crying bitterly, downstairs and left me with my big sister, telling her not to let me upstairs again.

Mammy discovered when I went to school that I was just as willing to sing on any occasion. One day, when Daddy came in from work at six o'clock, I said, 'Do you want to know something that happened in school today?'

He said, 'If you wait until I sit down.'

Mammy was smiling and said, 'Be prepared.'

I said, 'Sister Teresita asked if anyone in the class could sing *The Sash My Father Wore*. She said she was from Great Yarmouth and she would like to hear it. I put my hand up and said I could. And so I sang it. She gave me some sweets and asked where I had learned it. I said a girl who lived in our street sang it until I learned it. *I can sing a whole lot of songs. My family all sing.* She thanked me and said I was a very good singer but she didn't ask me to sing anything else.'

My Daddy took a fit of coughing and I got him a glass of water. I told him Sister Teresita often took a fit of coughing and she always drank some water.

The Tea Party

When I was a child, we lived in Springwell Street. We had a shop; actually it was where the Grouse Inn is now. When I was about nine years old the shop was converted into a parlour, one of the reasons being that Daddy was working in McHenry's to keep seven of us – and the shop. There was a high level of unemployment at the time, and Mammy, being very kind-hearted, gave groceries where there was need, saying, 'Pay me when times are better.' Mammy was not a good business woman.

The parlour was kept for important visitors. But there couldn't have been many important people calling, because nearly everybody walked straight into the kitchen.

Most nights my Uncle Bobby and Daddy's two uncles, Tommy and Mickey Killough, would visit. They'd talk about football and politics. Daddy had two rules – no scandal and no bad language. Everything else was fine. But it wasn't of much interest to a girl of nine. So one night Mammy said I could bring my three cousins Marie, Pat, and Nellie in to play in the parlour.

Santa had brought me a tea set and Mammy had allowed me some biscuits and milk to make it real. My brother Tommie, whom I usually allowed to play with us, wanted to be in the fun. But I said, 'No, boys don't play wee houses.'

Tommie said, 'I'm not leaving,' and sat down on the settee.

I said, 'I'll get Mammy for you and she'll make you move.'

'She won't,' he said. 'She told me I could come in, and anyway, I live here too.'

I had set the tea set out on a wee table and I had just enough milk and biscuits to do the four of us, and Tommie was spoiling everything. My cousins had old hats and handbags and were anxious to begin the fun. 'Pretend you all have come to visit me and we'll have the food. Just ignore Tommie, nobody cares about him anyway.'

With that, Tommie lifted the milk jug and jumped onto the big chair at the side of the fireplace. He looked into the mirror above the mantelpiece and said, 'Will you have some milk with your tea?' in a high-falutin voice.

I was raging. 'You shouldn't be here,' I shouted, and ran across the room. I grabbed his ankles and the next thing he was lying on the floor and the jug was lying beside him in pieces.

I started to cry and knelt down to lift the broken jug. Marie said, 'Your Tommie isn't moving. Maybe he's dead.' I looked at my brother's white face and closed eyes.

I said, 'I'll have to get my Daddy.' My cousins decided it was time to go home and I went in alone to tell the news. I went into the kitchen past Mammy who was knitting, and went to Daddy's side. I caught his sleeve and said, 'I think I've killed Tommie. He's in the parlour.' Mammy and Daddy made for the door, the uncles close behind.

I fled upstairs and crept in below the bed in the attic. I was normally too afraid to go in there on my own. But it was nothing to the fear of what Mammy and Daddy would say about me killing Tommie.

I had begun to learn the piano and I knew I was going to be a great pianist. It might take a few years but it would happen, of that I was sure. Now everything was changed. The piano would have to be forgotten. I started to bargain with God. 'If you let Tommie be alive again, I'll stop playing the piano. Honestly, I'll do without being famous; just make him able to get up. I didn't mean to kill him, but you know yourself, he was asking for it. You can even break one of my fingers so that I'll have some pain.' I was going to say 'break them all' and then thought that that would be a bit much.

At that moment, Anna lifted up the edge of the quilt and peered at me. She said, 'You're in for it. Mammy's raging.' I started to cry. She said, 'You shouldn't have done it you know, but I won't tell you're up here. I have to go down again now for I'm at my homework.' I cried louder. Anna turned back and lifted the cover again. She said, 'If you find an aniseed ball in there, it's mine. I dropped it a week ago.' And with that she went off.

I waited a while and then decided to go down and find out about the funeral. I said, 'God, I'm going downstairs now. Don't let Mammy kill me and don't let Daddy be cross with me for he liked Tommie, I suppose because he was called after him.'

I crept down the stairs and stood outside the kitchen door listening. I could hear voices but I couldn't hear what they were saying. I pushed the door open a wee bit and looked in.

And what do you think, there was the dead Tommie, sitting on a wee creepie at my Daddy's feet. He was supping ice cream with a contented look on his face. In those days, you could take a cup to McGroggan's and they filled it with ice cream for tuppence. It was a great treat.

I was very, very cross. I had been worried enough to be giving up the piano and the cause of it was having the time of his life. Tommie had just been slightly concussed and nobody had given a thought to me.

A Night at the Fireside

It was a night near the end of the school holidays. Mammy was sitting on the sofa knitting. She never sat idle as far back as I can remember. On this particular night, five of the seven of us were present.

It was that time of the evening when it was neither light nor dark. Daddy had been reading. It was how he spent most of his spare time. My brother Tommie and I finished playing a game of Ludo, which I won. Tommie didn't want another game.

He went down to the scullery and brought up water in an old basin. He said, 'Are you right, Daddy?'

Daddy glanced up, gave a wee smile and said, 'I suppose so.'

That was all Tommie needed. As quick as he could move, he brought a towel, which he put round Daddy's neck. Then with a comb he dipped in the water, he started to comb Daddy's hair. He would comb it all down and then back up.

Every time he did this, I always sat on a wee creepy and cleaned the fluff from the turn-ups of Daddy's trousers.

My Cousin's Gift

One day, when I arrived home from school Mammy said to me, 'Hurry up and eat your dinner and get your homework done 'til you see what I have for you.'

It wasn't my birthday and it wasn't Christmas so I had no idea what was in store. I finished both in record time and said 'I'm ready.'

She opened a brown paper bag and said, 'There you are.'

I gazed at what I thought was the most beautiful dress I had ever seen. It was pale lilac satin with puff sleeves. I said, 'Why did I get it?'

Mammy said 'Pull it on you until I see what it's like.' I did so and it was a perfect fit.

I asked, 'Is it new?' I was the youngest of the four girls and very often I wore my sisters' hand-me-downs, but I had never seen this gift before.

'Your Aunt Jeannie left it down for you,' I was told. My cousin Enda had grown out of it before she got any great wear out of it, so her Mammy gave it to me. I wore it to Sunday Mass and made up my mind to coax Mammy to let me wear it to school on Monday.

'You can not,' she said. 'You might get it soiled. It's not the sort of dress you could wear every day.' But I coaxed and coaxed.

On Monday morning, there was a wintry sunshine, and Mammy relented. I couldn't wait to get to school to show off my lovely dress. I was early that morning and when I entered the classroom my classmates were full of admiration. I was delighted. Just then the teacher entered. My face was wreathed in smiles; very soon they were replaced with tears.

The nun didn't like the dress. 'Stand out here,' she said. I did so. Her face tightened. 'Go now to the cloakroom and put on your coat,' she said. 'That garment is far too short, it is unladylike. It is shameless and I will not have you sitting in this room looking like that. My goodness,' she said, 'I can see your knees.'

I was heartbroken. I sat as quiet as a mouse when I returned from the cloakroom. I wished home time would come quickly.

When school was over I ran the whole way home. When I got there, I opened the kitchen door, and burst into tears. 'Teacher said she could see my knees,' I sobbed and the whole story came out.

I thought Mammy would be very angry with me or maybe Sister Vianney. But she looked at the sadness in my face, and said, 'Anna is going to Woolworths and I'll give her the money to get you the wee bangle you saw on Saturday.' If I had got it then I would have been delighted, but somehow that moment when I was told to put on my coat hurt badly. I was eight years old at the time, and I didn't know what was wrong.

That evening when Daddy came in Mammy told him about the dress. He looked at me for a long moment and then winked at me saying, 'I'll tell you this, I think it is a beautiful dress and you look a wee wheeker in it.'

I felt the pain in my heart ease. My Daddy's seal of approval was more important than what the nun thought. I only wore the dress on Sundays after that, and always kept my coat closed at Mass!

Living

When I was six years old, a classmate died and I still remember seeing her corpse. She wore a crocheted brown and orange dress and her face was freckled and her hair was fair with a hint of ginger, and straight. Her grandfather took her to and from school every day. He held her hand and carried her satchel. Once, when it snowed, he carried her on his shoulders. She was timid and shy and he did his best to shield her from harm.

Springwell Street

I remember a family who lived there. Their father was demobbed from the army with no job. There were four children and they ran about in their bare feet only wearing shoes on Sundays. The daughter had to go to Smith's round the corner, for thrupence worth of hard bread at closing time on Saturday evenings. But I never felt sorry for them, because they played in the street with the rest of us and they always seemed to be laughing. Many a time I heard my mother say she had never seen a doctor at their door.

Their father used to borrow the *Telegraph* from us. But he never read it until late evening when he would sit out on his windowsill. I was fully grown before I learned the reason for this. He hadn't a penny for the gas, so he waited until the lamplighter turned on the street lamp before he could find out what was happening in the rest of the world.

Concert

As the nights got colder the uncles gathered in our house and they would talk about football, the government and world events. My brother Tommie and I loved these times. We would crawl below the table and listen to all the arguments. The tablecloth covered us and we were often overlooked. We both thought Daddy knew everything about everything and one night when our eldest brother argued against him, we went to bed crying.

We loved music of all kinds and on Sunday nights we gave a concert for whoever was unfortunate enough to be visiting. We dressed up in old clothes and sang and told jokes. The highlight was dance music on the radio from eight-thirty until nine, when we would leap about all over the place. My mother was very patient and never objected. Daddy would often slip out, returning when the concert was ending, and he'd lament and say, 'Oh, did I miss it?' He was a good story teller and I loved the nights when it was just ourselves and we'd beg for a song or a story and ask for the gas not to be lit – just the glow of the fire.

One for the Pot

I was always amazed about how long Mammy was married and yet she never seemed to know how many potatoes or vegetables to put in a pot to make stew or soup for seven children and for herself and Daddy, for you could be sure Sheila or Nellie would have to go across to Nanny and see if she would oblige Mammy by taking a bowl of food, as Mammy, one more time, had made too much and it would be a sin to throw it out. And often Nanny would have said, 'There's two fresh sodas I baked this morning. Tell your mummy *thanks.*'

Housemaid's Knee

Mammy came in from a neighbour's house and said she had to go back, as the neighbour, Mrs Scott, was going into hospital. My brother Tommie was in the house with me. We had a shop at the time, and Mammy put the snib down on the glass door and told us to be good until she came back. She said Mrs Scott had housemaid's knee, and I said, 'I am never going to wash a floor when I grow up.'

I was terrified of doctors, nurses and hospitals. I slammed the big front door shut in case the ambulance would take me away as well. I thought they just filled it up with people. My mother and half the street had to call instructions to me through the keyhole, to get a chair, stand up on it and open the big door. Mammy was very cross with me and the commotion I caused.

Halcyon Days

Every year my Daddy rented a house in Waterfoot for the summer months. Those children in the family who were still at school had two glorious months of freedom. The two eldest had started work and so they stayed at home with Daddy until weekends, when they all joined us.

One particular summer we almost struck silver. Anna, Tommie, Maurice and I spent most of the time on the beach. Along with other children we played Rounders, Cricket or Leapfrog. Maurice, being the youngest, dug tunnels and made moats to his heart's content within sight of the rest of us.

However, one day the four of us were at a loose end waiting for others to join us. We were skimming stones when Anna, always the ringleader, suggested we should make paper boats and sail them at the bridge which was situated at the entrance of the village. Tommie was sent into the house for the necessary paper, Anna warning him not to say what it was for. It was the unwritten law that we would steer clear of the bridge, not that there was a lot of traffic, but there was no footpath, just a track at the side, down to the river.

Anna and I took Maurice by the hand and Tommie arrived out of breath.

'I hope Mammy has read today's paper, because it was the only one in sight and I had to hurry,' he said.

Anna said, 'If you had looked on the shelf in the scullery there was a pile of papers.'

Tommie was cross and said, 'I didn't have time and anyway Mammy was *in* the scullery.'

We made the boats and Anna made an extra one for Maurice. We dropped them over the bridge and raced to the other side to watch. We cheered and argued about whose was the first and then made another set of boats.

After the third set was launched Anna got very excited.

She said to Tommie, 'Keep a tight hold of Maurice's hand. I want to show Mary something and then I'll show it to you.' Leaning over the bridge she said, 'Mary, look to the right where the water disappears under the bridge, beside the clump of nettles.'

I did as I was told and said, 'I'm looking.'

'Do you see something shiny?' she asked.

I peered into the water and after a few minutes I said, 'Yes, what is it?'

'It's a lady's silver compact,' Anna said knowingly.

'Well, what about it?' I said.

Anna said, 'Don't be stupid! It's bound to be worth a lot of money. I bet it's an heirloom or something.'

'I don't suppose we'll ever know,' I said.

Anna looked at me in disbelief. 'Of course we'll know, when you bring it up.'

I was stupefied. 'But we're not allowed in the river.'

Anna said, 'Mammy never actually said so now, did she?'

'Well, a girl at school says there's sharks in the water!'

'She meant hundreds of miles out at sea, not in the river. You'd believe anything anybody told you,' Anna said.

Of course, I waded into the water.

Anna and Tommie, holding tight to Maurice, started calling out instructions. 'Over a bit. Up a bit. To the left. Come further up the river. Now! You're beside it. Now put your arm straight down.'

I did as I was told but failed to strike silver. 'I can't find it,' I called up.

'You're standing fair on it,' Anna shouted back.

I was trying to hold my dress up so that it wouldn't get wet, for then Mammy would know. I also wanted out of the muddy slime.

'Put your hand down again. Right, you're dead on it. Bring it to me.'

I stooped and lifted the priceless heirloom and brought it up to the bridge. Anna looked at me eagerly.

'Well, where is the compact?' she asked.

'Compact my eye,' I said. 'It's a tin lid off a can.'

We were so disappointed.

Maurice was warned and warned not to say where we had been. When finally we went in for tea, he said, 'Mammy we were good. We didn't go to the bridge to sail boats, and Anna didn't tell Mary to go in the river, and Mary didn't get a shiny thing either!'

We were banned from going next nor near the river for the rest of the summer.

Bowled Over

I loved the weekends. No school, and it seemed the weather was always good. We played skipping, two balls against the wall, hoops and sticks, and the boys played marbles, chestnuts and spinning peeries. Sometimes we joined together and then we could play Rounders, Sweep the Street, Lie Closer, which was really Tig, and Here's Two Men Coming to Seek Work.

The row of houses on the opposite side of our street had a long communal strip at the back which was called the yard. One particular evening, we gathered at Uncle Bobby's house, agreed to play Cricket, and we all trooped through his kitchen to the yard. Uncle Bobby was at a Summer League Football Match and Aunt Mary was visiting a friend who was sick.

We had a makeshift wicket and a bat of sorts and we started the game. We had seven players and to even it out we allowed our cousin Bridie, who was eight, to play.

Everything went well until my cousin Pat went in to bat. We allowed Bridie to bowl, explaining she had to try and hit the wicket. She did just that, and everybody started jumping up and down and cheering, but the celebration ended almost immediately. Pat was so angry at being put out by his wee sister that he threw the bat into the air in temper. It went clean through Mrs Gray's window, and the next thing she was out the back door screaming at us, 'Who threw that bat?'

Everybody ran into Uncle Bobby's house. Nellie quickly barred the door. Pat and Maurice ran upstairs and hid below the bed. Of Tommie and Jim there was no sign.

Mrs Gray was shouting in the window, 'I want to speak to your mother. I'm going to get the police.'

Nellie and I huddled in at the back door, but poor Bridie was terrified out of her wits and was standing up on the couch screaming, 'I don't want to go to jail.'

Aunt Mary arrived in the middle of the hysteria. She assured Mrs Gray the pane of glass would be replaced and calmed everyone down. I went over home to tell Daddy he had to pay half of the repairs.

Endearing Young Charms

The year I was twelve, I was singing a solo at the Glens of Antrim Féis. It was *Believe Me, If All Those Endearing Young Charms*, by Thomas Moore. I arrived off the bus and went looking for Sister Vianney, the nun who had taught me.

She was very flustered and said, 'For some reason, Moore's melodies are banned this year. However, I have seen the programme and I have chosen another song for you to sing. Come down to the beach with me and I will teach it to you before the contest.'

I said, 'Sister, do you think it might rain? Because I am wearing my new Jennywren Coat and my Mammy warned me not to get it wet.'

Sister Vianney looked at me as though I was mad, and said, 'Walk with me and listen carefully.' She had a tuning fork with her and every so often she would hit it on a stone and sing *low doh – high doh*. We walked and walked until she was content that I knew it well enough to sing it solo.

I won third prize and when I told the whole tale to my Mammy and Daddy, Mammy said, 'You did well. I'm proud of you.'

Daddy asked, 'Who got first?'

Mammy was raging at him.

Snow Mask

Snow presented problems for me as a child. I had eye trouble, which was always aggravated by snow. I couldn't bear the whiteness. I seem to remember missing school during snow-time but I know it was only if it lay for any length of time.

Once, my Daddy solved the problem, at least for that year. He had been in conversation with an American naval officer. During the talk, Daddy was telling him about me and how I couldn't face snow. As a result, the young officer brought him a black velvet mask which covered my eyebrows to below my nose, with two slits for me to see through.

I don't know where the sledge came from; I just know it was ours. The children from the surrounding streets gathered like magic, every one of them clamouring for a ride. I was in the midst of them, enjoying snow like everyone else!

I didn't want to come in that night. The air rang with childish voices claiming, 'It's my turn next. It's my turn!' And strangely enough, although the sledge was ours, every child felt they all had equal rights.

The only Asian people in our town at that time lived at the bottom of our street, and none of us children ever noticed they were different; after all they had the common denominator, Ballymena accents.

When the snow melted, I was still wearing the mask, which I wore to school and everywhere else outside. But one day I was sitting listening to the teacher reading a story when I tore the mask off my face, crying, 'I don't want to be different anymore.' The nun, Sister Vianney, persuaded me to put it on again until I'd go home.

To this day, I can't remember at all what became of the black velvet mask.

A Visit to Big John's House

As I finished my plate of stew my Mammy said, 'Take the basket and go up to Big John's. He said he has too many vegetables and if one of you would go up he'd fill the basket.'

'I've to go dancing at half six and I have my homework to do,' I said.

'You can be there and back in fifteen or twenty minutes,' she said. 'Go on with you now, you're not always as anxious to do your homework.'

'Can Anna not go?' I asked.

'Anna has to take the tea to your Daddy. What's wrong with you? Do as I tell you, away you go,' Mammy said.

I lifted the basket and went out muttering. I didn't want to go. Anna and I didn't like Big John. We were afraid of him, but we couldn't say exactly why. I think I was about twelve at the time.

I opened the gate and walked up the path to number 15. Maybe John's wife would open the door. But no such luck. John stood there.

'Come in,' he said. He stood to the side, letting me pass, as he turned and closed the front door. I stood in the living room clutching the basket to me like a suit of armour. John came in smiling, 'Come on through to the garden.' I followed him through the kitchen, a small scullery and a narrow passageway which led to the yard. Big John opened a door and we were in the garden. I felt like a fly when the spider invited him into his parlour.

He led the way down through the rows of vegetables. I said, 'You have a very big garden.' I was determined to hide my nervousness. 'Do you like growing things? Is your family not in? Do they help you?' 'Easy, Mary,' I said to myself, 'if Anna was here she'd say, *You're talking too much, be careful.*'

He was pulling carrots and leeks and putting them at his feet. Next, it was parsley and scallions. He moved towards the lettuce then stopped.

'Bring me over your basket and I'll put them in, while you go down to the bottom and pick some flowers for your Mammy.'

I saw him shaking the clay off as I moved towards him. The sun was in my eyes and suddenly I was on the wrong side of him. He stood between me and safety.

'I won't hurt you,' he said softly. My throat was dry, I was sick with fear. He moved towards me.

The next moment my feet, with a will of their own, took off. I could hear him thundering behind me. He was saying, 'I won't hurt you.'

'Dear God,' I prayed, 'help me. Please.'

His son Roy appeared at the top of the path. 'I'll cut her off at the top, Dad, you sweep to the left.'

I couldn't believe it. I thought he'd help me.

I was twisting and ducking through the garden, trampling on vegetables and plants. John's arm shot out towards me and as I screamed I heard a voice shout, 'This way, Mary, quick!' The youngest son, Jackie, who was a year younger than me was waving to me across the garden.

I raced past his father and Jackie came to meet me. Taking my hand we ran through the small gate into the yard. He said, 'Run on. Jump over the wall.'

I never looked back. I just kept running. When I reached home I was bathed in perspiration. I ran upstairs and closed the attic door, leaning against it. He wouldn't come up here. When I went downstairs, everything was normal. My Mammy said, 'Did you go to Wilson's?'

'I did, but I didn't get it. I forgot.'

'Well you can go tomorrow after school. Away to the dancing class now and come straight home.'

I told Anna in bed that night. She said, 'We'll never go inside that house again.' I couldn't remember us ever having been there before. Next day, Big John brought the basket saying I'd left it behind. I never told my Mammy, but I think she knew something wasn't right. I never had to go to his house again. He had a very bad drink problem and as Anna and myself were afraid of drunk men, we used that as a reason to not like him. We always left the kitchen when he came in. I never told anyone else about the garden.

Stage Struck

The Parish Bulletin stated: *There will be a meeting on Wednesday at 8 p.m. in the hall for those interested in Amateur Dramatics.*

I was brimming with excitement when I met my cousin Marie, who was also one of my best friends.

'We'll definitely audition, for we're both good at acting,' Marie said, with the confidence of youth.

I agreed. We had always been in the front row at school concerts, not necessarily because of talent, but more because of our enthusiasm, a fact which escaped both of us at the time.

We could talk of nothing else until Wednesday night. It never occurred to us that we wouldn't get a part, or, worse still, that only one of us might.

Miss Hill stood looking down from the stage at the expectant faces. There were about twenty-five of us.

'I thought we could begin with a play incorporating choral singing. The one I have in mind is called *The Upper Room*.'

There was a buzz of conversation.

Miss Hill spoke again. 'Let me explain a little about the play. It is about the Last Supper when Jesus met with the Apostles, and the events leading to His betrayal.'

After making this last statement, she waited a few minutes before continuing. 'I think you will like the play. Two of the main parts, Jesus and Judas, will be played by experienced amateurs I have worked with in the past, and the rest will be chosen from amongst yourselves. The people in the crowd scenes will double as the choir and as rabble-rousers off stage.'

There was much giggling, everyone shy, yet eager to be chosen. Marie and I left the hall full of talk. We were going to audition, that was for sure.

I said, 'Hasn't she a lovely voice, Marie?'

Marie agreed, saying, 'It's the sort of voice you just have to listen to.'

When I got home I told my family all about what had happened at the meeting. 'I'm going to try for a part,' I said. 'I think I'd be good at acting. There's a part for a young Jewish boy, who is a follower of Jesus. I'm going for that!'

My mother said, 'That's nice, but don't set your heart on getting a main part, Mary, just enjoy being in the play.' In the next breath she said, 'Everyone's had supper. Go down to the kitchen and get yours, then off to bed. It's late.'

Marie and I both auditioned for the part of the boy. Personally, I couldn't understand why Marie had bothered. Her blonde curly hair had always been much admired and the pale complexion that goes with that colouring seemed more evident now.

I, on the other hand, had black hair, which I wore in a fringe. In addition, I was swarthy-skinned, small and slightly built. I was that boy! It was the first time I was glad that Marie and I, though cousins, didn't look alike.

'Do you think I have much of a chance of getting the part, Mary?' Marie asked.

'As good as anyone else,' I said, lying through my teeth. Did she never look in the mirror I wondered? Even brown shoe polish wouldn't make her face look Middle Eastern and, even if it did, what would she do with her blue eyes? I mean, who had heard of a blonde, blue-eyed Jew? Certainly no one in Ballymena.

At home, I rehearsed and rehearsed in front of the mirror. But I felt I needed wider scope. I stood on top of the stairs, proclaiming, 'He is innocent! He is innocent!'

My Mammy appeared in the hallway.

'Are you all right, Mary?' she asked. 'Who are you talking to?'

I went into the bedroom and closed the door. Once more in front of the mirror I called, 'He is innocent! He is innocent!'

My sister put her head round the door.

'Are you sick or something? Every night you are stuck in this room, talking to yourself in the mirror. Does Marie do this at home?' she asked.

I was mortified. If she said anything to Marie, I'd die.

Now, looking at the polish I'd smeared on my face, she queried, 'What's that stuff on your face?'

'What stuff?' I parried, rubbing vigorously to remove it. Anna could be very annoying when she took the notion.

When I came out my younger brother was standing holding his hand to his brow, moaning, 'He is innocent! He is innocent!' I rushed past him to the bathroom. I locked the door and buried my face in a towel to stifle my sobs. No one understood how important it was for me to practise.

Next evening, on the way to the hall, I asked Marie, 'Do you rehearse in front of the mirror?'

'Not at all,' she answered quickly. 'Our ones would think I was daft. Do you?'

'No, not at all. It's not all that important,' I said. I hated the pretence between us. Before this, we had shared our secrets about everything.

The night came, at last, when Miss Hill was to make her choice. I'd be glad when it was all over. I just hoped Marie wouldn't be too disappointed.

When we were seated, she whispered, 'I'm really nervous.'

'So am I,' I said, then added, 'Good luck!'

At that moment I felt if the part of Judas had been up for grabs, I would have got it. I had all the qualities.

Miss Hill stood smiling in my direction.

'Well,' she said, 'I know you have all been very patient, so I'll get on with it. Mary, will you stand up please?'

Marie said, 'Congratulations!'

'Thanks,' I said, 'I only wish there had been two boys.' I meant it. I could afford to be generous. I just wished my Mammy could have been there. She'd have been so pleased for me.

Miss Hill put her arm around my shoulder. 'You have a lovely, clear voice, Mary,' she said. 'That's what made my decision so difficult.' I was trembling. Miss Hill was still speaking. 'And as I need a strong voice to lead the chorus, you were the obvious choice, Mary.'

What was the woman talking about? Had she taken leave of her senses?

'Marie, as it was between you and Mary, that means I've chosen you to play the part of the Jewish boy.'

For a brief moment, I saw pity in Marie's blue eyes, but, as I hugged her in congratulation, the pity vanished.

There was much clapping and talking at that point and I walked off stage.

The part I had coveted was of a boy proclaiming, 'He is innocent! Innocent!' The part I got was leader of the rabble, shouting, 'Crucify Him! Crucify Him!'

A Stranger

He must have thanked his lucky stars when he knocked on the door, that it was my mother who opened it.

'Can you tell me where I can find a room for the night?' he asked. 'I'm a stranger in town.'

We, the family in the living room, knew what was coming.

'Come on in and have a cup of tea. It's a terrible night.'

We were proved right. The stranger was soon seated at our hearth. Myles – he said that was his name – was from the West of Ireland. 'I'm looking for work,' he said. 'I'm told this is a good town for such.' Within moments he was enjoying tea and toast.

'Take off your coat and you'll know the good of it when you go out,' my mother said. Myles did so, with no coaxing. We listened while the stranger talked his way into our house. 'The two boys can go down to my mother's,' she said. 'It's no night to be looking for lodgings. It's pouring down.'

My brothers were not best pleased at having to give up their bed. But they knew there'd be no argument. They put on their coats and set off. When my father came home from the barbers, the stranger was already enthroned. What my father's thoughts were we didn't know, he being a very quiet man.

Myles McGrath got a job at Langford Lodge. And the boys still slept at Granny's.

'How long is he staying then?' asked my father at the end of a month.

'I don't like to ask him,' Mammy said. 'He's shy. Sure, he's finding his feet.'

'I've found them. Beneath our table,' father said wryly. 'He must look for somewhere else. The boys want to come home.'

She agreed. 'He'll be heartbroken,' she said. 'He said it was his home from home.'

'I'm sure he did,' my father said.

She sighed, 'I'll tell him tomorrow.'

Myles said he'd look for new digs. Two days later he was gone. A letter had come from Mayo, he had said, telling of his father's death.

Two weeks later my father asked if my mother had sent his brown suit to be cleaned as he couldn't find it in the wardrobe. For a second there was silence. Then Mammy said, 'Well, Myles couldn't go to his father's funeral without a suit, could he? And I gave him a shirt and tie and your old overcoat,' she added. 'I felt sorry for him and him going to his own father's funeral. But he is going to send them back afterwards.'

My father smiled and sighed in a strange way. 'The greatest of these is charity,' he said.

Myles McGrath never returned, nor did my father's clothes. When we talked about it afterwards, not one of us could remember the stranger receiving a letter.

Growing Pains

My brother was being married in Dublin. This seemed to be the signal to my mother for all sorts of changes in our lives. 'We'll have to paper the house from top to bottom, in case some of them want to come up and visit,' she said. My father pointed out that they were hardly going to come straight after the wedding. It made no difference; Mammy's heart was set on papering.

'They will all have to get new rig-outs,' was her next comment.

Daddy said, 'Whatever you say.' He knew he had lost the battle, even before it had begun.

My brother, Joey, was the eldest; then four girls, of which I was the youngest and then two younger boys. Joey had got a job in the Northern Bank and my parents were very proud of him. I was so pleased with the comment about new rig-outs. I being the youngest of four girls meant that a lot of my clothes were handed down, but not this time. I was delighted. I was going to move towards growing up.

I was to have my first perm and my outfit was bought in the Adult section of Goorwich's Fashion Store. The coat was green with a light tan herringbone, a straight line and an inverted pleat in the back. The big decision was shoes. 'Oh you'll definitely have to wear a bit of a heel with that coat,' Mammy said, 'and nylon stockings and I saw a lovely pale green dress as I was coming out of the shop and now that I see the coat in daylight, that dress will just set it off.'

I was so excited, I couldn't believe my ears. Maybe I was going to get court shoes. At last I was being allowed out of laced-up shoes and knee socks. My sister Anna would be amused, I was sure. She was three years older than me and we had a love/hate relationship. Anna hated it when Mammy would say to her, 'If you're going to the pictures, take Mary with you.' I was a bit of a 'Miss Goody Two Shoes' and Anna had discovered boys and I cramped her style.

Just then Mammy broke into my thoughts, saying, 'Mary, are you going to stand there 'til the 13th April? Away upstairs and put that coat on a hanger.'

Unfortunately I wasn't quite out of earshot when Mammy said to Daddy, 'Mary is at that awkward age. She's neither child nor woman, and it's hard to dress her.' I fled upstairs, for fear that Daddy might agree.

We went shopping for shoes. It seemed court shoes were a bit too grown up for my feet. I had to settle for Cuban heels. Then we bought nylons. I thought maybe Mammy might be proved wrong.

The next step was my first perm. The hairdresser asked, 'What sort of a perm do you want, dear?'

'Mammy said I was to get a good one, about thirty shillings. Please don't make it fuzzy. I'd like it soft please.'

She smiled with a funny gleam in her eyes and proceeded to wash my hair, digging her nails into my scalp. The next thing she was putting about fifty wee tight curlers in my hair. She put a net on and led me to a dryer. It was set at too hot a temperature and I twisted and squirmed, hoping it would soon be over.

Then I got a handbag. It was the beginning of a lifelong romance. Anna used to say, 'Are you sure you haven't that bag in bed with you?'

Two of my aunts decided to travel to Dublin early on the day before the wedding. They said that Anna and I could travel on the train with them. Mammy was delighted as it meant less of a squeeze in the hired cars that were taking the rest of the guests. I was very excited. I'd never been further than Portrush before.

Nobody thought to give me a hairnet, and as a result, I wakened in a great frizz. My lovely green felt hat wouldn't sit down on my head. I was in floods of tears. My two aunts were in separate rooms, so Anna took charge. She said, 'Come on, dry your tears. I'll fix it.' She marched me into the bathroom and stuck my head beneath the cold tap. She soaked it thoroughly and told me to straighten up. I stood up dripping wet but hopeful. Anna patted it lightly with a towel, stuck my hat on my head and said, 'Now get those Cuban heels and we'll show these Dublin folk a thing or two about style.' We were very naïve.

The two aunts emerged from their rooms dressed to kill, and we made our way to the church. I hobbled along, going over on my ankle every so often. The shoes were definitely not a success.

Nor, it transpired, was the perm. During the wedding reception my perm dried, and this meant the hat sat on my head like a green pea on the top of Slemish Mountain. The seating plan at the reception had placed Anna on the opposite side of the room to me. Every time I looked at her, she was smiling broadly at me and waving. I was very emotional and crying because my big brother was getting married and leaving home. I thought Anna was trying to cheer me up. I didn't discover until afterwards that the sight of me, perm gone wrong, my hat sitting on top of a dried-up frizz and me crying, reminded Anna of Stan Laurel.

On the way back to the hotel, I confided to Anna that I was sure I had done myself some injury because I couldn't step up the footpath, and found I could only take small short steps when walking. When we reached the hotel Anna said, 'Walk across the room to see if I can find out what is wrong with your legs.' I did as she told me. She collapsed on the bed laughing.

'You eejit,' she said. 'You didn't take the stitching out of the knife pleats in the back of your dress. Little wonder you couldn't walk!'

So two major things happened that 13th April – my brother got married and I learned it took more than Cuban heels and a perm to make me an adult.

The Facts of Life

I was born into a world of secrecy with regards to the 'facts of life'. My mother, like other mothers, thought there was little need for such information. My sister Anna, who was three years older than me, didn't agree with this and so she busied herself during her teen years trying to prize the information out of female relatives who were slightly older. My eldest sister, Nellie, was the prime target. 'Nellie,' she said one day, 'Mary and I know nothing about boys and life and things like that and you were Granny's favourite. Did she tell you anything that you can tell us?'

Nellie said, 'The only thing Granny ever told me was that if I met a jealous man I was to cross the street.'

'Well did Great Aunt Susie tell you anything?'

'Aye, she said *If you get a man keep a bit of yourself to yourself. I never got one but if I had I would have known what to do.*'

Anna wasn't at all enamoured with this.

There were four girls in our family and when the second eldest, Sheila, got married, Anna was sure she had struck oil. However Sheila gave the usual answer, 'You'll find out soon enough.' No one, it seemed, was willing to talk. Anna decided to make her own rules.

Weird and mad they were but I followed them religiously and well.

When she herself was getting married I was her bridesmaid. She asked her husband-to-be about the best man, 'Is your brother Frank OK?'

'Aye,' says Charlie, 'Mary will be fine.'

But then a friend met Anna down the town and she said to her, 'Mary would need to keep an eye on that Frank fella.' Anna didn't ask any questions.

The arrangement was that Frank was to take me to the pictures in Belfast after Charlie and Anna had left on their honeymoon. Anna didn't want to frighten me but she said, 'Mary, no matter what happens, don't take your hat off.'

So of course Frank and I had something to eat and then into the Ritz Cinema. There I sat with my corsage of flowers pinned to my jacket with my handbag and gloves on and the crowning glory, my far-from-small hat.

As the film began Frank whispered, 'Would you not like to take your hat off?'

I said, 'No fear, and I'm going to tell Anna!'

He bought ice cream in the interval, but I didn't take any. I sat clutching my handbag for dear life and the perspiration poured from my brow. For a time many's a lad must have wondered why I always took a hat with me on a date.

When I came to be married I was still short of facts. Anna, like the rest, told me nothing except, 'God, you'll know soon enough.' I never did discover what the hat had to do with anything.

a Couple of Swells

I remember when I was about eighteen. It was a Saturday evening and my parents and two of my sisters and two of my brothers were all in the house. We had had our normal Saturday evening tea, a great big fry. Daddy was sitting at the top of the table and everybody was laughing and talking. There was a lovely warm glow. It was early summer and the fire was backed up with slack to heat the water. Mammy came up the floor carrying the teapot. She had on a dress and a half apron with small flowers all over it. The talk was about marriage and Daddy said he wouldn't mind if we all stayed with him and Mammy and never got married. I remember thinking, wouldn't it be great.

We had a great big wall clock and it was ticking away furiously on the wall. The smells of bacon and soda bread were heavy in the air. My Mammy said something about Daddy not wanting us to have the happiness they had. And Daddy said, 'They couldn't be as happy as us.'

The radio was on in the background playing *We're A Couple of Swells*. Daddy took Mammy by the arm and danced her up the floor singing and us all joining in. Mammy had always told us about Daddy being a great dancer; the Waltz, Foxtrot and

Quickstep. She herself had never been to a dance. Granda had been a very strict man with regards his three daughters. So when Daddy danced her up the floor she was in fits of laughter at her own attempt to dance.

I remember thinking how lucky I was. My eldest brother was married and so was my sister Sheila. But I was eighteen and had no notion of marrying. I loved to dance and that was it.

That particular day stayed in my mind for a long time, because none of us could know that on 30th September Daddy would be dead. He was admitted to hospital a week beforehand for a stomach operation. His blood pressure plummeted and he died four days later. He died in hospital and Mammy and my eldest brother Joey were with him at the time.

I remember when she came home from the hospital, Anna and I hid in the bedroom, because we didn't know what to say and we were afraid she would be different. Life changed that day. We were put into black, which we wore every day for a year. We were not allowed to play the wireless, nor were we allowed to go dancing, or to the cinema.

My mother was genuinely heartbroken.

Eventually, when we told Joey that Mammy wasn't eating properly and no longer seemed interested in anything, he decided to speak to the Doctor. The Doctor visited us and said to Mammy that she had to start looking after us again. She said, 'Do you not know my husband is dead and I don't care if I die too?'

He told her, 'Your children have lost a much-loved father.' He pointed out that it might be a different pain but nonetheless horrendous to take in. 'Your children need your strength to help them cope.' He also told her that in return it would, eventually, help her.

Responsibility

When our father died, my brother Tommie and I decided that we would have to look out for Maurice, who was the youngest. There were seven of us and I felt we had had the benefit of the others steering us through those times when we were sure we'd never laugh or love again.

The thing was, Maurice, who was eleven at the time, wasn't really all that keen to be led. That first Christmas after Daddy died was going to be very hard, so it was important we would all be looking out for Mammy. Maurice had always been expert at getting money for sweets from Mammy, but now she only had the widow's pension. My father's wages were eight pounds per week, the widow's pension, ten shillings – a huge difference.

Tommie noticed that Maurice was whispering in her ear more than usual. He said to me, 'I don't know what he is up to but she always gives him something from her purse.'

We tackled him about it. He said we didn't need to know what it was for.

We had our own suspicions but when we asked Mammy, she said, 'Och, let him alone, he misses your Daddy. Anyway, he never gets more than a thrupenny bit.'

However we both felt awful on Christmas morning when Maurice gave Mammy a box of mint chocolates wrapped in Christmas paper, and he said, 'That's what I wanted the money for. Mrs Gray said she would keep them for me, and she wrapped them up for me. I know Daddy always brought you mints, and us sweets, every Saturday night.'

Dancing the Night Away

From an early age Maurice was very independent and short-tempered, but he never held a grudge.

On his way home from school on his fourteenth birthday he called in at McHenry's, the place my father had worked in for thirty years. He asked the boss for a job.

The boss asked him if Mammy knew he was applying for one. He said, 'Your parents wanted you to go to the Tech.'

Maurice said, 'I hate school and anyway my Mammy needs the money. I am leaving school whether you give me a job or not. I'll get work somewhere.'

Brian McHenry asked him, 'When were you fourteen?'

Maurice replied 'Today is my birthday.' It was the 22nd September.

Mr McHenry said, 'You will have to wait until the end of the quarter, which will be after Christmas.'

Maurice asked him was he going to give him a job. The answer was *yes* and Maurice came home and said, 'I've got a job in McHenry's and I start after Christmas.' Despite Mammy and her brother, Uncle Pat, trying to talk him into going to the Tech, they didn't succeed. Maurice started work in January.

A group of us in the Parish asked if we could start up a dancing class as there were lots of people wanting to learn. We were given permission but we had to make some rules. There were nine of us and we set up a list which we all agreed to implement.

First – if you had a boy/girlfriend you could only dance with them twice in one night.

Second – no alcohol was allowed.

Third – you could not coach one person all night.

Fourth – no 'Blackout' waltzes.

You had to circulate so that everyone would have a fair chance of learning the steps.

We were pretty strict about the rules. The females were anyway. A few of the male members liked the girls they danced with to be good-looking and datable. However, by the end of the year almost all could dance though there were broken romances all over the place; a high price to pay, some thought, to learn *slow, slow, quick, quick, slow*. Still, Victor Sylvester had nothing on us.

Maurice learned to dance and got on well but I drew Tommie's attention to the fact that he always and only danced the girls I knew on the team. I said to Tommie, 'If he keeps doing that I'll have no friends left.'

Tommie talked to him, saying now that he could dance maybe he should dance me more and let the other team members have a change. Tommie said, 'Mary won't mind,' and I agreed.

So the next dance we were going to Tommie said, 'You know we want you to enjoy yourself and you are doing well. Just remember what we said and you will be fine.'

I joined in saying, 'Remember, if a girl asks you to dance in a Ladies' Choice, whether you have danced her before or not, you must return it by giving her the next dance, that's *protocol*.'

'I hear you, I hear you,' he said, and went to stand on the other side of the hall, across from us.

He danced me the first four dances. He was like lightning on the floor, quick as a flash. I wasn't in a steady relationship at the time and would have liked to see who might ask me to dance, but Maurice was on the ball too quickly. Just then the M.C. called a Ladies' Choice. I walked over to ask Maurice and he said, 'Och Mary, that wee blonde was just about to ask me.'

I said, 'Maurice, you've danced me all night. I couldn't ask anyone else.' I went back to my friends quite annoyed with him when the M.C. called the next dance. I couldn't believe my eyes. After all we had told him, Maurice had given the return dance to the blonde!

On the way home Tommie blasted him for not doing as we had told him. And I said, 'If it hadn't been for Dessie Glynn I'd have been left like the last rose of summer, Maurice. You never listen.'

Maurice exploded. 'Do you see you and Tommie, you know it all! I'm sick to death with you both. *Do this, do that, dance this one* and *don't dance that one! Make the girl feel at ease, ask her if she is enjoying herself and what does she think of the hall.* I did all those things and she just nodded her head and said *Yes* and *No*. Eventually I remarked *It's very warm, isn't it?* and she said *Will I get my coat?* You didn't tell me how to answer that.'

We were speechless.

The Night Before the Wedding

It was the night before the wedding and Vincey, my husband-to-be, and I were on our way back from delivering the cake to the hotel in Cushendall. Vincey smiled at me and said, 'I have to get you home before twelve, isn't that right?'

'Yes, it's bad luck for you to see me after midnight.'

He laughed and said, 'Is that for always? That's going to be awkward.'

We drove in silence for a while and Vincey said, 'Is anything wrong? You're very quiet.'

I said, 'I'm fine.' But I wondered what he'd say if I told him 'I feel afraid. I don't really know you, not the real you. We've never talked about serious things and here I am about to join my life with yours, for better or for worse.'

I mean, I didn't know how much he earned, whether he liked children or not and all those sorts of things. I kept glancing at him; he seemed older, different somehow.

I went into the house when he dropped me off and had a cup of tea and a chat with Anna and Mammy.

The night Vincey proposed sprang into my mind and made me smile. 'I was thinking maybe we could get engaged,' said Vincey. We arranged to go to Belfast the following Saturday to buy the ring. Vincey said, 'We'll tell nobody until we come home again.' I agreed. Then I told my Mammy, and she told my aunts, my sisters and my brothers. They were, of course, told it was a secret.

On the Friday night, before the big event, I called at my brother Tommie's house. His wife Eileen invited me in and in the course of the conversation said, 'Tommie was saying you're getting the ring tomorrow.'

I said, 'Nobody is supposed to know.'

Eileen said, 'I've told nobody, don't worry.'

Then she said, 'Are you excited? What sort of ring are you thinking of?' I said I hadn't a clue. Eileen said, 'I always had a good idea of what I wanted. I mean, have you thought of three or five stones or maybe a solitaire. Or will it be diamonds or sapphires?'

I said, 'I honestly haven't thought about it,' and Eileen replied, 'Well you'll need to think about it soon. I always knew I wanted one with a shoulder.'

At this point Tommie came into the room saying, 'Don't fret about it. Sure Vincey and you can discuss it on the way to Belfast tomorrow. It'll be grand. I'm delighted for you. Vincey's a good fella.'

I thought about what Eileen had said. She had mentioned a shoulder. What in the name of heaven was a shoulder? I decided that probably Tommie was right; Vincey and I would sort it out on the way to Belfast.

When he arrived for me the next morning, however, he must have got a shock. My Aunt Lizzie, sister Nellie, brother Maurice along with my Mammy were all ready to wish us well on our day's outing. They stood on the doorstep waving. Vincey had hired a car from Adam Ervine, a local car dealer. He turned the ignition key and the engine spluttered and died. He did this a few times and each time the farewell delegation on the doorstep waved their goodbyes. Vincey and I were red with embarrassment. After four or five tries the car started. We were on our way.

We talked about this and that but no mention of the ring, price or number of stones. I thought, 'When we get to Addlestones I'll look in the window, and Vincey can go ahead into the shop and arrange with the shop assistant what price range to show me.' But when I stopped so did Vincey. I had no choice but to go inside.

I watched from Vincey to the assistant to see if they made eye contact or signs but they didn't, so obviously there was no secrecy needed. Vincey said, 'We'd like to see some engagement rings,' and we were shown into a little booth.

The assistant asked if I had a preference for three or five stones, or perhaps a solitaire. I said, 'Not really.'

The young man continued, 'I'll just measure your finger first and then I'll bring a tray of rings for you to choose from.'

I said, 'I think I don't want a solitaire.' In my mind I had decided they were probably very expensive. Then it struck me what Eileen had said so I said very clearly, 'Oh and I want one with a shoulder.' That would show him I knew all about rings!

I glanced at Vincey. The poor fellow was very quiet and the perspiration was glistening on his forehead. I decided to get it over with as quickly as possible.

I liked the second ring I tried on and decided there was little point in dallying, so I said, 'This is lovely.'

Vincey smiled and said, 'Good, that's it. As long as you like it, that's grand.'

We drove to Bangor, had a meal and a walk along the seashore. When we came home Mammy had organised a surprise party for us. Vincey looked at me and smiled. Everything was all right.

Remembering this, I realised it would be the same loving, kind, good-tempered man I was marrying in the morning. We had the rest of our lives to discuss things and find out about each other. I knew everything would be grand. We could talk. Well, I would. Vincey would probably just listen!

Mary Higgins has given us all something precious. She has given us her life. There is nothing clichéd about her evocation of growing up in Ballymena. It is true to its genesis: to the hurts; the fears; the passion; the breathless pleasures of being young. The stories are made rich with foresight and hindsight and she has that great gift of knowing what will elicit spontaneous response. She knows what not to say. She is the child in 'Sing It Loud' marvelling at her own irrepressible enthusiasm, or in 'A Night at the Fireside', quietly picking fluff from the turn-ups of her father's trousers. She is able to give us her family, especially her parents, and we feel reassured that the world really does contain such extraordinary people.

COVER PAINTING: Beverley McCord

AUTHOR PHOTOGRAPH: Peter Higgins

ISBN 978-0-9560995-3-2

Price:
£7.00 €10 $12 US

SUMMER PALACE PRESS

ISBN 978-0-9560995-3-2

9 780956 099532